ADULT SKILLS Literacy for Living

Applications and Forms
Book 1

Written by Dr Nancy Mills and Dr Graham Lawler

The Adult Skills Range

The range of Adult Skills resources has been developed by Aber Education in response to needs expressed by tutors, students and governmental agencies. The materials are appropriate for adults who require support in advancing their literacy and numeracy skills.

Dr Nancy Mills, Adult Literacy/Numeracy author and editor, has over 25 years of combined experience in the adult education areas of teaching, tutor training, developing curriculum resources and publishing. Dr Graham Lawler, Adult Literacy/Numeracy author and editor, has over 27 years of combined experience in the adult education areas of teaching, tutor training, developing curriculum resources and publishing.

Applications and Forms – Book 1

ISBN 978-1-84285-119-7

© 2009 Aber Publishing

P.O. Box 225

Abergele

Conwy County LL18 9AY

Published in Europe by Aber Publishing. www.aber-publishing.co.uk

Cover illustration by Michelle Cooper. Typesetting by Jonathan Bennett and Aber Publishing.

Contents

© 2009 Aber Publishing – Adult Skills   Forms – Book 1

Introduction

Tutor's Notes

Adults who seek help with literacy/numeracy have different motivations. Some want to get a job, apply for a driver licence, do personal banking, qualify for a loan - activities that require the completion of applications or forms. This resource has been created specifically to assist students with these skills.

Filling out some applications and forms can be daunting even for the most educated person. For an adult who does not have strong literacy and/or numeracy skills, being asked to complete an application for employment, driver licence or even a library card can cause frustration, aggravation and failure.

The purpose of Book 1 is to provide a variety of applications, forms, and frequently asked questions that are encountered in everyday adult lives. The pages can be copied and used for practice, or the appropriate answers can be discussed and the vocabulary defined.

In the Vocabulary section, a brief introduction precedes the list of common and/or hard-to-understand terms for each separate application or form to make it easier for you to incorporate them into your lessons. The words are listed in columns and should be read from left to right. With only a few exceptions, they are in the same order as they are found in the applications.

This can also be a significant support resource for your lessons based on this subject. Copy the pages that complement your instructional materials.

Photocopiable resources

The following is a list of some of the ways in which photocopiable teaching resources (blackline masters or BLM) may be used in an instructional environment to ensure variety of presentation and moderation in photocopying costs.

- Copy the selected pages to A4 paper for each student to form a booklet. Students write to the sheet.

- Copy the resource to an OHP transparency/ scan to a powerpoint display and project it on the wall for class discussion.

- The lists of vocabulary words and duplicated questions lend themselves to one-on-one or small group discussion activities.

- Present a copy of the selected page(s) to students the day before the exercise to become familiar with the types of questions they will be answering.

- Use peer tutoring by presenting the resource to one student to work with another.

Teachers please note:

- Please ensure that students are aware that Cambriana is a fictional country for the purposes of compliance with copyright law.
- It is NOT intended that students work through all of these forms without direction. The purpose of this book is to provide realistic learning activities for students.
- Make sure students are aware that DOB refers to date of birth, and NI refers to National Insurance (number).
- Colleagues should also be aware that the army application simulation contains personal questions. It may be advisable to separate male and female students for this activity.
- Make sure that students understand the nature of applying for a phone service in that people often apply for a new phone service before they move into the new property, hence the need for two addresses on the form.

Vocabulary

Driver Licence Application   Pages 12-15

Whether or not your students already have a driver licence, this form has vocabulary and questions that are commonly asked on applications.

Vocabulary

application	licence	surname
personal details	supporting identification	suitable documents
previous	provide	donate organs
event	next-of-kin	date of birth ____/____/____
residential address	postal address	Day Month Year
notify	telephone number	recorded on the database
support	evidence	original identification
expiry date	if applicable	identity
licence class and type	vehicle	evidence of address
restricted licence	full licence	learner licence
affect your ability to		medical condition
drive safely	adversely affect	diabetes
double vision	Alzheimer's	epilepsy
fits	head or spinal injuries	high blood pressure
amputations	mental illness	joints or limb problems
stroke	convulsions	worsened
diagnosed	related to eyesight	renewal date
contact lenses	knowledge and belief	correct
disqualified	signature	captured
entitled to access	may request correction	readily retrievable information
attached	after receipting	detach bottom sheet
failed		

Driver Licence Test

Whether or not your students already have a driver licence, the application for a driving licence is good practice. It also has many words commonly found on other application forms.

Vocabulary

form	completed an application	endorsement
surname	date of birth ____/____/____	personal details
recorded on the database	Day Month Year	
notify	residential	
contact telephone number	optional	
full licence	restricted licence	older driver
theory	my best knowledge and belief	disqualified
obtaining or holding	signature	appointment
evidence of identity	reverse of this form	conducting or supervising
practical	normally	advise
cancellation	excludes weekends public holidays	

© 2009 Aber Publishing – Adult Skills   Forms – Book 1

Answer these questions

1   What does 'personal details' mean? _____

2   What does 'residential address' mean? _____

3   If you notify someone it means you tell them something, TRUE OR FALSE _____

4   What is an 'amputation'? _____

5   What is a 'disqualified driver'? _____

6   What does 'documents supporting identification' mean? _____

7   What is your signature? _____

8   What does 'evidence' of address mean? _____

9   What does 'next-of-kin' mean? _____

10 What does d.o.b. mean? _____

My son got his licence when he was 17. As a reward for his hard work I bought him his first car and three days before his 18th birthday he was dead. He was driving far too fast and took a corner badly. He skidded and went into a tree, killing himself and his three mates in the car with him.
His mother still cries for him and I still blame myself for buying that car.
Please learn from this, don't do this to your family!

Vocabulary

Employment Application 1   Pages 14 – 15

Applications for employment are fairly generic except for information that is relevant to the specific position and company. You may have a collection of employment application forms that you can use to supplement these two.

Vocabulary

establishment	indicate dates	location
reason for leaving	surname	address
phone, private	most recently attended	highest qualification attained
enrolled	two most recent jobs voluntary basis	work performed on a
work experience	company	job title
supervisor	dates worked from - to	suffered
sensitivity or allergy to	ligament/tendon sprain or injury	Repetitive Strain Injury
chemicals	back problems	answered
any of the above	claim	disease or ailment
work performance	regular attendance	health and safety
provide details	contact	relationship to you
convicted of a criminal offence	excluding misdemeanours or traffic violations	charges pending
describe in full	not necessarily	bar you from employment
minimum number of hours	maximum number of hours	successful
correct	to the best of my knowledge	omission or erroneous information
grounds for instant dismissal	accordance with company policy	authorise the supervisors
offered employment	Employment Contract	commencement of work
smokefree	comply	statements
signature	submission	considered
reapply		

Employment Application 2   Pages 16 – 17

Vocabulary

office	warehouse	maintenance
personal details	telephone, private	telephone, mobile
address	postal (if different)	birth date D/M/Y
emergency contact name	relationship	legal work status
legally entitled	work permit	health
conditions	ability to effectively carry out	functions and responsibilities
position	court convictions	convicted
criminal offence	legal proceedings	hearing
education	secondary	tertiary
institution	qualification gained	certificates
work experience	jobs held	beginning

Vocabulary

most recent employer	continue on separate sheet	company
position held	dates employed	brief description of duties
reason for leaving	referees	character references
seek	confidential information	authorise
information sought	released by them	ascertaining my suitability
signature	additional	successful
indicate	explain	believe
qualified	declaration	

Cambriana Army Application   Pages 18 – 22

The 'Application for consideration for a career with the Cambriana Army' needs long discussion. In lieu of reproducing the entire application for a real army like the British Army, we have listed a number of the questions that appear on the form for one-to-one or class discussion. Ensure students are aware that Cambriana is a fictional state that is used here to avoid copyright issues.

Vocabulary

convicted	criminal offence	court proceedings
court hearing	court martial	asthma
severe headaches	migraines	currently
provide details	surname	dependants
defence	highest qualification	in support of
professional	technical	vehicle
academic awards/ distinctions	opportunity	appeals
situations	events	background
personal strengths	selected	aspects
personal situation	extra-curricular activities	shortcomings
may diminish your chances	centimetres	corrective/contact
consulted a doctor	medical treatment	sensitivity to chemicals
fortnight	disability	pension or compensation
existing condition	prior	rejected
deferred	vaccinations	enlistment
abnormal shortness of breath	coughed	swollen or painful joints
spinal injury	disc trouble	sciatica or lumbago
recurrent	indigestion	vomiting
passing	STD	abnormal
anxiety or panic attacks	psychological	mental disorders
concussion	unconsciousness	fainting
sinus	partially	defective
motion	complaint	severe reaction
injection	patient	hospital
conditions	previously mentioned	

College Training Application   Pages 23 – 24

Applying to attend a tertiary training institution such as an FE college or just to enroll in a course is an important skill and something that adults usually do independently. Having the confidence to do it often makes the difference between applying and not applying. This is a typical (generic) application form using a fictitious college as an example.

Vocabulary

enrolment procedure	personal details	legal surname
previous name	postal address	mobile phone
email address	citizenship	permanent resident
British	International	language
specify	secondary education	qualifications
attended	highest academic award	GCSE Certification
Certificate	University Entrance	A Level Certificate
required to complete	subject	unit standards
details	gained	employment details
previously	employed	currently
full-time	complete	position
work experience	brief details	most recent
employer	supplementary	describe
programme	inform yourself	careers
strengths	not covered	hobbies
effects of injury	long-term illness	disability
may interfere	accommodation	authorisation
signature		

Power Supply Application   Page 25

When going flat hunting or purchasing a home for the first time, an application must be made for power supply. This application asks some different questions from most of the others.

Vocabulary

complete	field	speed up
opening your account	asterix	indicates
mandatory	account details	date of birth
joint account holder	residential address	suburb
province	property	landlord
property usage	domestic	commercial
evening	mobile	electricity
currently	supply	commence
supplier	instructions regarding	meter
describe location	garage	current meter reading
meter number	standard terms and conditions	

Vocabulary

Telephone Connection Application   Pages 26 – 27

This form, as many others, can be completed online. This is a hardcopy of the online application for telephone service. You may want to discuss online application forms with your students, and how they often have drop-down boxes for selecting dates, etc.

Vocabulary

connection	relevant	fields
continue	marked with an *	given names
surname	address	suburb
postal address (if different)	current	contact number
area code	mobile prefix number	additional
information	optional	completing
previous occupant details	property	directory listing
preferred	published	available
directory assistance	non published	confidential
indicate	smartphone services	

Library Membership Application   Page 28

Students should be aware that in addition to books, library members have access to many other services. For example, they can borrow DVDs and CDs, use the Internet and even attend free courses. There are many questions you could ask or discuss with students about this application.

Vocabulary

library	membership	male
female	surname	middle name
date of birth	street address	postal address
notification	reserves	fines
languages	alternative contact	eg
neighbour	etc	relative
employer	relationship	receive
information	categories	fiction
reference material	non-fiction	magazines
periodicals	orientation programmes	conditions
issued	responsible	returning borrowed items
renewed	incur fines	expire
consecutive	conditions of membership	overleaf
signature	patron type	present your card
visitors	returning borrowed items	expire
two consecutive years	change of address	cancellation
loss, theft or damage	activity on your card	notified
cancel	suspension of borrowing rights	outstanding
unpaid	reserved	overdue
reminder	replacement cost	resume
unreliable	debt collection agency	

Vocabulary

Keeping a Diary   Pages 29 – 30

This page has three different pages from diaries, plus a page for Names and Addresses. Photocopy them and let students practise using the different types. Or, white out the dates and copy pages of one type of diary to make a small diary for each student, which they can use to document their daily activities. The Diary Details Worksheet gives information that students can place in the appropriate places on the diary pages. The information will need to be reduced so the meaning is clear and fits in the space provided.

Vocabulary

Monday	Tuesday	Wednesday
Thursday	Friday	Saturday
Sunday	January	February
March	April	May
June	July	August
September	October	November
December	appointments	telephone
address	business	mobile

Medical Centre Application   Pages 31 – 32

On the first visit to every doctor's office or medical centre, the patient is asked to complete a form similar to this one.

Vocabulary

primary health organisation	enrolment	practice
dependants	surname	NI number
residential	for office use only	Community Services
High User Health Card	ethnic group	please state
declined	authorise	practice register
disclose	receive government funding	obtain copies
previously attended	on behalf of	lifestyle
questionnaire	complete	finalised
medications	allergic	approximate
illnesses (all items on the list should be understood)	operations (all items on the list should be understood)	alcohol
accident	exercise	eg
average week	amount	influenza injection
tetanus immunisation	history	deceased
pregnancy	cervical smear	abnormal
mammogram	medical	advertisement
newspaper	recommended	

Generic Visa Application   Pages 33 – 34

This type of application includes questions not often found on common forms. Some questions will be quite challenging but offer excellent learning opportunities.

Vocabulary

© 2009 Aber Publishing – Adult Skills   Forms – Book 1

Vocabulary

visa

section

place of birth

religious name

sex

widowed

expiry

correspondence address

previous travel

deported

act of terrorism

war crimes in the
  course of armed conflict

true and correct to the
  best of my belief

  entry

type of print

valid

nationality

professional name

marital status

separated

place of issue

mobile telephone

outside your home country

removed

organisation

certify

false or misleading statement

signature

answers in ink

family name

maiden name

aliases

divorced

passport

permanent home address

spouse

refused entry

criminal convictions

crimes against humanity

furnished

permanent refusal

mm/dd/yyyy

© 2009 Aber Publishing – Adult Skills   Forms – Book 1

Applying for a Provisonal licence

In Cambriana, like many countries, you have to apply for a provisional licence.

You can apply for your first Cambriana provisional driving licence online if you:

* are a resident of Great Britain or Cambriana

* can meet the minimum age requirement

* can meet the minimum eyesight requirement

* are currently not prevented from driving for any reason

* can pay £50.00 by Mastercard, Visa, Maestro, Electron, Delta or Solo debit or credit card

* have a valid UK passport or another form of identity

* can provide addresses of where you have lived over the last three years

© 2009 Aber Publishing – Adult Skills   Forms – Book 1

You must send us:

- Your completed application form

- a medical certificate from your doctor

- Proof of Liability Insurance:

- Proof of liability insurance includes providing insurance documents such as:

- DMV form DL-123;

- or an original liability insurance policy binder;

- or an insurance card with: your name, policy number, issue and expiration date.

- The liability insurance documents must show your name, the effective date of policy, the expiration date of the policy, and the date the policy was issued.

- Even if you do not own or drive a currently registered vehicle you may still apply for a license, but a restriction will be placed on your driver license. This restriction limits you to only driving "fleet vehicles" and costs £10.00 when you are ready to remove it from your license.

Acceptable Proof of Identity Documents:

1. Valid, unexpired Driver License or State-Issued Identification Card

2. Certified or original birth certificate.

3. Original Social Security card.

4. Official School Registration records signed by a school official and Diplomas/ certificates issued by schools, including secondary schools, community colleges, colleges and universities.

5. Unexpired Military Identification, including DD-2, DD-214, Common Access Card, and. Military Dependents Card.

6. Valid, unexpired Passport from any nation.

7. Certified marriage certificate from a Register of Deeds or appropriate government agency .

8. Valid, unexpired documents issued by the Cambriana Bureau of Immigration Services (BIS).

9. Court documents from Cambriana. jurisdiction.

10. U.K/Cambriana Veterans Universal Access Card.

Cambriana: A safer place to Live

Application for a Driving Licence

Application Type check one

1 ☐ Driver's Licence   2 ☐ Learner's permit and driver's licence   3 ☐Motorcycle Provisional Licence

---

If you are applying for a replacement licence check one of the following

☐ My current licence is now out of date

☐ My current licence is unavailable because it is ☐ lost   ☐ stolen   ☐ Destroyed or mutilated

Applicant Information

Name _____   _____

Address _____

Post Code_____ NI Number_____

Telephone: private (   ) _____   work (   ) _____

DOB_____**Are you under 18? Yes ☐ Parent/guardian signature required. No ☐**

Parent Name_____ **Parent Sig**_____

Answer the following Questions

If you answered yes to any of the above, was a government disability claim made?	☐ Yes	☐ No
1 Do you wear Contact Lenses or spectacles?	☐ Yes	☐ No
2 Do you have a physical or mental condition which requires you to take medication?	☐ Yes	☐ No
3 Have you ever had a seizure, blackout or loss of consciousness?	☐ Yes	☐ No
4 Do you have a physical condition condition which requires the use of special equipment in order to drive	☐ Yes	☐ No
5 Have you been convicted in the last ten years of any offence concerning a motor vehcile?	☐ Yes	☐ No
6 Has your licence ever been revoked, suspended or disqualified?	☐ Yes	☐ No

---

Required tests   Passed Failed   Remarks/Paid Stamp Enter customer Number

Vision

Theory test   Payment Made   Cheque £49.99 To Cambriana

Prac test   ID Confirmed ☐   DVLC

For DMV use only, do not write below this line

Forms – Book 1

Driver Licence

Class 1, 1L and 1R

Car licence. Includes tractors or combinations of vehicles which have a gross laden weight (GLW) or gross combined weight (GCW) of 4,500 kg or less; mopeds and all-terrain vehicles, forklifts with a GLW of 15,000 kg or less.

Note: Tractors are not suitable for practical driving tests.

Class 2 and 2L

Includes any rigid vehicle with a GLW of more than 4,500 kg but less than 15,001 kg; any combination vehicle with a GCW or 12,000 kg or less; any combination vehicle consisting of a rigid vehicle with a GLW of 15,001 kg or less towing a light trailer; any rigid vehicle with a GLW of more than 15,001 kg with no more than 2 axles; and any vehicles covered in Class 1.

Class 3 and 3L

Includes any combination vehicle with a GCW of more than 12,000 kg but less than 25,001 kg; and vehicles covered in classes 1 and 2.

Glass 4 and 4L

Includes any rigid vehicle (including any tractor) with a GLW of more than 15,000 kg; any combination vehicle consisting of a rigid vehicle of GLW more than 15,000 kg towing a light trailer; and vehicles covered in classes 1 and 2, but not class 3.

Class 5 and 5L

Includes any combination vehicle with a GCW of more than 25,000 kg; and vehicles covered by classes 1, 2, 3 and 4.

Class 6, 6L and 6R

Motorcycle licence. Includes mopeds and all-terrain vehicles.

Evidence of Identity

These must be original documents:

- UK or Cambriana Passport or overseas passport that is current or has expired within the last 2 years or
- UK or Cambriana Passport driver licence or overseas driver licence that is current or has expired in the last 2 years or
- Certificate of UK Citizenship or Cambriana citizenship or
- Certificate of identity issued under the Passports Act 1992 that is current or has expired in the last 2 years or
- Confirmation of residence permit issued on behalf of the Government or
- Refugee travel document issued on behalf of the Government that is current or expired in the last 2 years or
- Police or Defence Force photo-identity card issued to non-civilian staff that is current or expired in the last 2 years or
- Full birth certificate issued in UK, Cambriana or Europe
- Firearms licence containing a photograph issued under the Arms Act 1983 that is current or expired in the last 2 years or
- Certificate of identity issued under the Immigration Act 1987 that is current or expired in the last 2 years.

Privacy Information

The particulars specified on the Application for Driver Licence test will form part of the Driver Licence Register. Collection and dissemination of this information is authorized by the Land Transport Act 1998. Under the Electoral Act 1993, s.263B, the Land Transport Safety Authority (LTSA) is authorised to release information for data matching purposes to the Electoral Enrolment Centre. The Privacy Act 1993 provides rights of access to, and correction of, any retrievable personal information held by the LTSA. Should you wish to exercise these rights please contact the Transport Registry Centre, LTSA, Private Bag, Cambriana or email info@ltsa.govt.cam. Information relating to driver licence status (but not your signature) may be released under the Land Transport Act 1998.

Employment Application 1

Application for Employment

Have you ever worked at this establishment before? ☐ Yes ☐ No

If yes, indicate dates, location and reason for leaving.

_____

Name _____   _____

Address _____

Telephone: private ( ) _____   work ( ) _____

School most recently attended:

Name _____ Phone ( ) _____

Address _____

Highest qualification attained _____

Now enrolled? ☐ Yes   ☐ No If yes, what class/form are you in? _____

Two most recent jobs:
(If you have not been employed, list any work performed on a voluntary basis or work experience.)

1. Name of company _____ Phone ( ) _____

   Address _____

   Job title _____ Dates worked From _____ To _____

   Supervisor _____

   Reason for leaving _____

   (Results of mgmt check _____)

2. Name of company _____ Phone ( ) _____

   Address _____

   Job title _____ Dates worked From _____ To _____

   Supervisor _____

   Reason for leaving _____

   (Results of mgmt check _____)

Have you suffered from any injury such as the following: (please tick appropriate boxes)

☐ hearing loss   ☐ Occupational Overuse Syndrome

☐ sensitivity or allergy to chemicals   ☐ back problems

☐ ligament/tendon sprain or injury   ☐ other _____

If you answered yes to any of the above, was an ACC claim made?   ☐ Yes   ☐ No

© 2009 Aber Publishing – Adult Skills   Forms – Book 1

Employment Application 1 (continued)

Do you suffer from any disease or ailment, which may affect your work performance or regular attendance at work, or the health and safety of yourself or others? ☐ Yes ☐ No

If yes, provide details. _____

Person to contact in case of sickness or injury:

Name _____ Home phone (   ) _____ Work phone (   ) _____

Address _____

Relationship to you _____

Have you ever been convicted of a criminal offence (excluding misdemeanours or traffic violations), or do you have charges pending? ☐ Yes ☐ No

If yes, describe in full. _____

(A conviction will not necessarily bar you from employment.)

Hours

What is the minimum number of hours you wish to work each week? _____

What is the maximum number of hours you wish to work each week? _____

What hour could you begin work? _____

How late could you work? _____

List any days you could not work (eg weekends). _____

How do you plan to travel to and from work? _____

If your application is successful, when could you start work? _____

1. I certify that the information contained in this application is correct to the best of my knowledge and understand that any omission or erroneous information is grounds for instant dismissal in accordance with company policy.

2. I authorise the supervisors listed above to give you any and all information concerning my previous employment.

3. I understand that if I am offered employment I will be required to sign an Employment Contract before commencement of work.

4. This company is a smokefree workplace. Should I be offered employment, I agree to comply with this policy.

Sign this application if you understand and agree with the four statements above.

Signature _____ Date _____

Your application submission will be considered active for 60 days. After that, you must reapply.

© 2009 Aber Publishing – Adult Skills   Forms – Book 1

Employment Application 2

Job Application for Cooper's Van Lines

Position applied for (you can tick more than one):

Office ○ Warehouse ○ Driver ○ Maintenance ○ Sales ○

Other _____

Personal details

First Name _____ Phone: private ( ) _____

Last Name _____ Phone: work ( ) _____

Address _____ Phone: mobile ( ) _____

_____ Birth date (D/M/Y) _____/_____/_____

Postal (if different) _____

Emergency contact name _____ Relationship _____

Legal work status

Are you legally entitled to work in UK?   Yes ○   No ○

Expiry date of work permit _____

Health

Do you have any health or other known conditions which may affect your ability to effectively carry out the functions and responsibilities of the position you are applying for?

Yes ○   No ○

If yes, please give details:

_____

_____

Court convictions

Have you been convicted of a criminal offence, or had legal proceedings made against you in the last five years?

Yes ○   No ○

If yes, please give details: _____

_____

Are you currently waiting for the hearing of any court charges? Yes ○   No ○

If yes, please give details: _____

_____

Education

Name of secondary or tertiary institution _____

Year of study (From – To) _____

Level and Qualifications gained (eg GCSEs, BTEC Eng., GNVQ) _____

_____

Employment Application 2 (continued)

Work experience

Please list all jobs held, beginning with the most recent employer, on a separate sheet.

Dates employed From _____ To _____

Company and position held _____

Brief description of duties and reason for leaving: _____

_____

_____

List any certificates, courses or additional information that would suit you working in this company.

_____   _____

_____   _____

Referees

Please provide details of at least two people we may contact for work experience or character references.

Name _____

Company _____   Telephone Contact: Work _____

Position of referee _____   Telephone Contact: Home _____

Name _____

Company _____   Telephone Contact: Work _____

Position of referee _____   Telephone Contact: Home _____

I agree that you may seek confidential information about me from the referees I have listed above and authorise the information sought to be released by them for ascertaining my suitability for the position applied for.

Signature _____ Date _____

Additional information

If your application is successful, when are you able to start? (D/M/Y) _____/_____/_____

Please indicate the hours and days you are able to work: _____

Why would you like to work for this company? _____

_____

Briefly explain why you believe you are qualified for this position. _____

_____

Declaration

I _____ (print full name) declare that the information contained in this application is accurate, complete and correct. Should my application be successful, the information will form part of my agreement of employment, and falsification or withholding of information may be grounds for dismissal.

Signature _____ Date _____

Cambriana: A safer place to Live

Application for consideration for a career in the Cambrianan Army

Name _____

Address _____

_____

Telephone: private ( ) _____ work ( ) _____

Email address_____Mobile Phone Number_____

Postal address if different from Address given above

_____

_____

School most recently attended:

Name _____ Phone ( ) _____

Address _____

_____

Highest qualification attained _____

Now enrolled? ☐ Yes   ☐ No If yes, what class/form are you in? _____

DOB_____ Gender_____ Ethnicity_____ (e.g. British, English,
Welsh, Scottish, Irish)

Do you have a driver's licence? Yes ☐ No ☐ If yes please provide your driver's licence number

_____

Are you interested in a full or part-time career?

Full ☐ Part-time ☐

Are you or have you ever been a member of:

Officer cadets Yes ☐ No ☐   Terrirorial Army Yes ☐ No ☐

If yes please give details of commanding officer

Name_____ Address _____

© 2009 Aber Publishing – Adult Skills   Forms – Book 1

Cambriana Army Application

"Your answers to the following questions will NOT necessarily affect your eligibility for the Army. Providing these answers will help us structure the application questions to suit you."

1. a) Have you ever been convicted of a criminal offence? (Do not include speeding tickets or speed
    camera fines unless they resulted in court proceedings.)   ☐ YES   ☐ NO
       If yes, provide details:

    _____

    b) Are you awaiting a court hearing? If yes, provide details.   ☐ YES   ☐ NO

    _____

    c) Have you ever been convicted by a court martial? If yes, provide details.
       (Note: begin each question on a new line with no number.)

    _____

2. Do you have, or have you ever had, or have you ever been told you have asthma?   ☐ YES   ☐ NO

3. Do you have or have you ever had severe headaches or migraines?   ☐ YES   ☐ NO

4. Are you currently married?   ☐ YES   ☐ NO

    If yes, please provide details of where and when you were married. _____

5. Have you ever been known by any other first or surname?   ☐ YES   ☐ NO

    If yes, please provide details. _____

6. Do you have any children or dependants?   ☐ YES   ☐ NO

    If yes, please provide details of your children or dependants.

    _____

    _____

7. Have you read the Cambriana Defence Force Drug Use Policy?   ☐ YES   ☐ NO

8. When did/are you leaving school? Age: _____   Year: _____

9. What was or will be your highest qualification upon leaving school?

    _____

10. Indicate which qualifications you have in support of your application. Please circle the correct
    answers.

    secondary school   tertiary   professional

    technical   vehicle licences   other _____

11. Provide details of any educational or academic awards/distinctions you received at school/
    university/college

    _____

    _____

12. If given the opportunity, what studies would you be interested in doing?

    _____

© 2009 Aber Publishing – Adult Skills   Forms – Book 1

Cambriana Army Application

13. What appeals to you about a career in the Army?

_____

_____

14. Describe any situations, events, background or personal strengths you believe will improve your chances of being selected.

_____

_____

15. Describe any other events, information or aspects of your personal situation that may affect your application.

_____

_____

16. Give details of your extra-curricular activities (eg sports, hobbies).

_____

_____

17. Describe any shortcomings you have that you think may diminish your chances of selection.

_____

_____

18. Enter your weight in kgs (e.g. 85 kgs) _____

19. Enter your height in metres and centimeters. (eg 1.74m) _____

20. Do you wear glasses or corrective/contact lenses? ☐ YES ☐ NO

21. Have you consulted a doctor in the last 12 months? ☐ YES ☐ NO

    Provide details. _____

22. Are you receiving any medical treatment at present? ☐ YES ☐ NO

    Provide details. _____

23. Have you ever been unable to work due to sensitivity to chemicals or dust or for other medical reasons? ☐ YES ☐ NO

    Provide details. _____

24. Have you ever had more than a fortnight off work due to an illness or injury? ☐ YES ☐ NO

    Provide details. _____

25. Do you have any illness, disease or disability at present? ☐ YES ☐ NO

    Provide details. _____

26. Have you ever received, applied for or do you intend to apply for a pension or compensation for an existing condition or prior disability? ☐ YES ☐ NO

    Provide details. _____

27. Have you ever been rejected for or deferred medical or life insurance? ☐ YES ☐ NO

    Provide details. _____

© 2009 Aber Publishing – Adult Skills   Forms – Book 1

Cambriana Army Application

28. Vaccinations - please advise if you have been vaccinated for the following:

    ☐ Diphtheria   ☐ Hepatitis A Hepatitis B
    ☐ Measles, Mumps, Rubella (MMR)   ☐ Polio
    ☐ Tetanus

29. Have you ever been medically examined for military enlistment?   ☐ YES   ☐ NO

    Provide details. _____

30. Have you ever experienced abnormal shortness of breath?   ☐ YES   ☐ NO

    Provide details. _____

31. Have you ever coughed up blood?   ☐ YES   ☐ NO

    Provide details. _____

32. Do you have or have you ever had swollen or painful joints?   ☐ YES   ☐ NO

    Provide details. _____

33. Do you have or have you ever had a backache, spinal injury, disc trouble, sciatica or lumbago?   ☐ YES   ☐ NO

    Provide details. _____

34. Do you have or have you ever had any knee, ankle or joint injury?   ☐ YES   ☐ NO

    Provide details. _____

35. Have you ever broken any bones?   ☐ YES   ☐ NO

    Provide details. _____

36. Do you have or have you ever had recurrent indigestion or a stomach ulcer?   ☐ YES   ☐ NO

    Provide details. _____

37. Have you ever experienced vomiting of blood or passing of blood?   ☐ YES   ☐ NO

    Provide details. _____

38. Do you have or have you ever had problems with bedwetting?   ☐ YES   ☐ NO

    Provide details. _____

39. Have you ever had a sexually transmitted disease (STD?)   ☐ YES   ☐ NO

    Provide details. _____

40. Are your periods abnormal? (Females only.)   ☐ YES   ☐ NO

    Provide details. _____

41. Do you suffer from or have you ever suffered from depression?   ☐ YES   ☐ NO

    Provide details. _____

42. Do you have or have you ever had anxiety or panic attacks?   ☐ YES   ☐ NO

    Provide details. _____

43. Do you have or have you ever had psychological or mental disorders?   ☐ YES   ☐ NO

    Provide details. _____

© 2009 Aber Publishing – Adult Skills   Forms – Book 1

Cambriana Army Application

44. Have you ever suffered from a head injury, concussion or unconsciousness? ☐ YES ☐ NO

    Provide details. _____

45. Have you ever had fainting attacks or blackouts? ☐ YES ☐ NO

    Provide details. _____

46. Do you have or have you ever had fits, epilepsy or 'turns'? ☐ YES ☐ NO

    Provide details. _____

47. Do you have or have you ever had nose, sinus or throat problems or illness? ☐ YES ☐ NO

    Provide details. _____

48. Do you have or have you ever had hay fever? ☐ YES ☐ NO

    Provide details. _____

49. Are you deaf, partially deaf or have you ever suffered from defective hearing? ☐ YES ☐ NO

    Provide details. _____

50. Do you have or have you ever had ringing in your ears? ☐ YES ☐ NO

    Provide details. _____

51. Do you have diabetes? ☐ YES ☐ NO

    Provide details. _____

52. Do you have or have you ever had problems with your eyes? ☐ YES ☐ NO

    Provide details. _____

53. Have you ever suffered from motion or travel sickness? ☐ YES ☐ NO

    Provide details. _____

54. Have you recently experienced weight loss? ☐ YES ☐ NO

    Provide details. _____

55. Do you have or have you ever had any skin complaint? ☐ YES ☐ NO

    Provide details. _____

56. Do you have or have you ever had a severe reaction to any food,
    drug or injection? ☐ YES ☐ NO

    Provide details. _____

57. Have you ever had an operation or been a patient in hospital? ☐ YES ☐ NO

    Provide details. _____

58. Do you have other medical conditions not previously mentioned? ☐ YES ☐ NO

    Provide details. _____

CollegeTraining Application

Northwest Community College
Enrolment Procedure

I. ▷ **Personal Details:**

Mr [ ] Mrs [ ] Miss [ ] Ms [ ]   Home phone [ ] _____

Gender M [ ] F [ ]   Work phone [ ] _____

Date of birth _____/_____/_____ _____   Mobile phone [ ] _____

Legal surname _____   Legal first names _____

Previous name _____   _____

Postal Address _____   Email address _____

British Passport Number _____

II. ▷ **Citizenship:** British [ ]   UK permanent resident [ ]   Irish [ ]   International [ ]

III. ▷ **Language:**   Is English your first language? Y N   If no, specify. _____

IV. ▷ **Secondary education and qualifications**

Name of the last secondary school you attended: _____

What was your last year at secondary school? _____

What is the highest academic award you hold from a secondary school? (Tick)

[ ] No secondary qualification   [ ] GCSEs (1 or more)

[ ] A levels (1 or more)   [ ] University Entrance

[ ] Non A-level courses   [ ] Other (specify) _____

UK students are required to complete this section.

School Certificate/Year 11/GCSE's

Subject	Year	Result

A-Level Certificate

Subject	Year	Result

Other qualifications

Subject	Year	Result

Details of any other awards, certificates or qualifications gained:

V. ▷ **Employment Details**

Have you been employed previously? Y N

How many total years have you been employed? _____

If you are currently in full-time employment, complete the following:

Employer's name _____

Your position _____

Address _____

_____

Phone _____

© 2009 Aber Publishing – Adult Skills   Forms – Book 1

College Training Application

Northwest Community College

If you have had any full or part-time work experience (other than above), give brief details, starting with the most recent.

Employer	Type of work	Years employed	Full/Part?	Hours/week

VI. ▷ **Supplementary Details**

Write brief notes to describe:

1. Your reasons for wanting to study on this programme;
2. The type of work you hope to be doing after you complete the programme;
3. The steps you have taken to inform yourself about careers in this area.

_____

_____

_____

_____

What are your strengths not covered by any of the above questions?

_____

_____

What hobbies, sports or other interests do you have?

_____

_____

Do you live with the effects of injury, long-term illness or disability, which may interfere with your studies? Y N

Describe: _____

VII. ▷ **Accommodation**

Do you require accommodation? Y N

VIII. ▷ **Authorisation**

_____   _____

Signature   Date

© 2009 Aber Publishing – Adult Skills   Forms – Book 1

Power Supply Application

New Customer Application

To apply for power to be connected, complete the form below. Please fill in every field to speed opening your account.

An asterix (*) indicates a mandatory field.

Account details

Last name		First name(s) in full	
Title		Date of birth	

Joint account holder details (as will appear on your account)

Last name		First name(s) in full	
Title		Date of birth	

New residential address

Number and street

Suburb/town

City/province

Do you own the property?   YES   NO   If no, please state landlord's name:

Property usage   ☐ domestic   ☐ commercial   ☐ both

New postal address (if different from above)

New contact details

Phone - day   Phone - evening   Phone - mobile

Fax   Email address

Date you are moving into your new house

Supply details

For supply of   ☐ gas   ☐ electricity   ☐ both

Is the electricity currently on? YES NO

If NO, when do you want supply to commence?

Present power supplier   Present gas supplier

Meter Reading Details

Where is your electricity meter?   ☐ inside ☐ outside ☐ other _____

If outside, describe location   ☐ front ☐ back ☐ garage wall ☐ other _____

Do you have a dog? YES NO   Is your dog tied up during the day? YES NO

If no, please enter instructions regarding your dog: _____

Enter your meter number and current meter reading:

Meter number		Current reading	

Gas meter details

Where is your gas meter/s?   ☐ inside ☐ outside ☐ other _____

If outside, describe location   ☐ front ☐ back ☐ garage wall ☐ other _____

Enter your meter number and current meter readings:

Meter number		Current reading	

☐ I have read and agree with the power company's standard terms and conditions of energy supply.

Signature_____   Date _____

Telephone Connection Application

New Connection Order Form

Please fill in the relevant fields

Your Details Given Name

Address where phone is to be connected

Your Current postal address if different from above

Contact Details: Your Contact Number

Please select listing type

Published ☐ *will be available in white pages, yellow pages and online*

Not published ☐ *this number will not be listed in any directory*

Library Membership

Library membership is free to all residents.

1. Male ☐   Female ☐

Surname ....

First name(s) ....

Middle name(s) ....

Date of birth...

Street address..

....

(for notification of reserves or fines)

Postal address ....

....

Email address

....

Home phone number ....

Daytime contact number ....

Do you read books in languages other than
English or Welsh?   Yes   No   If so, which
language?

....

2. Alternative contact - name someone at a
different address from your own, eg friend,
neighbour, relative, or employer, etc. who
could help us to contact you if you have moved.

Name of contact ....

Relationship to you ....

Home phone number...

Daytime contact number ....

3. Would you like to receive library information of
interest to you?   Yes   No

If yes, tick the boxes for the categories you
would like to receive information about.

☐ fiction   ☐ reference material

☐ non-fiction   ☐ courses

☐ DVDs   ☐ Bookmobile

☐ CDs   ☐ book clubs

☐ visiting speakers

☐ large type or recorded books

☐ magazines and periodicals

☐ orientation programmes

CONDITIONS OF MEMBERSHIP

1. You must present your card every time you wish to check out items.

2. No more than 40 items may be issued on your card at any time.

3. Visitors' cards are limited to five items at a time.

4. You are responsible for any items issued on your (or your child's) card.

5. You are responsible for returning borrowed items on time.

6. Items returned or renewed after the due date will incur fines.

7. Your membership will expire if you do not use your card for two consecutive years.

PLEASE REPORT AS SOON AS POSSIBLE:

- change of postal, residential or email address.
- cancellation of membership.
- loss, theft, or damage of borrowed items.
- loss or theft of your library card - if your card is lost or stolen, you are still responsible for any activity on your card until the library is notified to cancel it.

Suspension of borrowing rights will occur.

- when fines or charges have been outstanding for more than three months.
- when unpaid fines and/or charges reach $5.

EMAIL AND POSTAL NOTICES

1. You have the choice of being notified about reserved or overdue items either by email or by post.
   - The first reminder notice is sent by email when an item is three days overdue, or by post when an item is 10 days overdue.

2. The library will send two email/postal notices before charging the replacement cost of items not returned.

3. The library will resume sending notices by post if an email address is unreliable.

4. The library accepts no responsibility for notices sent but not received or read.

5. Lost items
   - If an item issued to you (or your child) is not returned to the library, you will be charged the replacement cost.
   - If lost item and/or overdue charges are not paid, your details will be sent to our debt collection agency.

Keeping a Diary

January 2019

Wednesday 13

8:00 _____
9:00 _____
10:00 _____
11.00 _____
12.00 _____
1.00 _____
2.00 _____
3.00 _____
4.00 _____

Thursday 14

8:00 _____
9:00 _____
10:00 _____
11.00 _____
12.00 _____
1.00 _____
2.00 _____
3.00 _____
4.00 _____

April 2019

17 Monday
_____
_____

18 Tuesday
_____
_____

19 Wednesday
_____
_____

20 Thursday
_____
_____

21 Friday
_____
_____

22 Saturday
_____

23 Sunday
_____
_____

March 2019

	Appointments	Things to do
6 Monday		
	_____	_____
	_____	_____
	_____	_____
	_____	_____
7 Tuesday		
	_____	_____
	_____	_____
	_____	_____
8 Wednesday		
	_____	_____
	_____	_____
	_____	_____
	_____	_____

Names and Addresses

Name _____
Address _____
_____
Home ( ) _____ Office ( ) _____
Mobile _____ Fax ( ) _____
E-mail _____

Name _____
Address _____
_____
Home ( ) _____ Office ( ) _____
Mobile _____ Fax ( ) _____
E-mail _____

Name _____
Address _____
_____
Home ( ) _____ Office ( ) _____
Mobile _____ Fax ( ) _____
E-mail _____

Forms – Book 1

Diary Details Worksheet

Read each piece of information. Identify the key information eg date, time, place, etc. Write onto the diary page only the essential information so you know what is meant and it fits into the space.

1. ....Dentist appointment on Wednesday at 1:00 pm

2. ....Take car in for MOT on Friday.

3. ....Job interview at 10:00 am on Thursday.

4. ....Call the vet for an appointment Duke's injection.

5. ....Pick up Jamie from work at 5:00 pm

6. ....Buy flowers for Mum's birthday.

7. ....Get blood test any weekday morning before 9 am

8. ....Visit Jane in hospital to see new baby.

9. ....Collect parcel from courier after 3:00 pm

10. ....Take tablets each day at noon for a week.

11. ....Meet with insurance agent at 11:00 am on Tuesday.

12. ....Go with Ernie to look at new flat on Friday.

13. ....Ring plumber to arrange time for him to fix toilet leak.

14. ....Ring Telecom to cancel phone service by end of week.

15. ....Buy food for family BBQ for Sunday.

16. ....Take ring in to jeweller to resize - needed before wedding on 20th.

17. ....Pick up college application for computer course.

18. ....Complete student loan application before the 15th.

19. ....Check movie times for Saturday night.

20. ....Get cash from bank before Saturday night.

Medical Centre Application

Name of GP _____

Practice name and address _____

List everyone in your family, including dependants, who you wish to enroll. If more room is needed, use the back of this sheet.

_____

_____

_____

Previous practice _____

Surname _____ First names _____ Gender F M

Date of birth _____ Practice ref Number _____

Residential address _____

_____

Postal address (if different) _____

Home contact number _____ Work contact number _____

Customer number (for office use only)

National Insurance number [_____]

Which ethnic group do you belong to? Tick the box or boxes which apply to you.

- ○ British
- ○ European
- ○ Other European
- ○ Australian
- ○ Irish
- ○ Asian
- ○ Tongan
- ○ Japanese
- ○ Black
- ○ Afro-Caribbean
- ○ Southern Hemisphere
- ○ Chinese
- ○ Indian
- ○ South East Asian
- ○ Other Asian
- ○ African
- ○ Latin American/Hispanic
- ○ Middle Eastern
- ○ Not stated
- ○ Declined
- ○ Other (please state) _____

By signing this enrolment form, I authorise:

- My name and personal details to be included on this practice register.
- This practice to use and disclose this information to receive government funding for my care.
- This practice to obtain copies of any health information about me from the practice I previously attended.
- My previous practice to disclose this health information to this practice.

Signed _____ **Date** _____

(For myself and on behalf of all dependants listed above.)

Health/Lifestyle questionnaire for new patients

Each new patient must complete this form before enrolment is finalised.

Full name: _____

1. Are you taking any medications?   YES   NO
   If YES, please list the medications you are on:

   _____   _____

   _____   _____

2. Are you allergic to anything?   YES   NO
   If YES, please name the things you are allergic to:

   _____   _____

3. Past medical history/lifestyle questions - please tick any of the following that you have and include approximate dates.

Illnesses	Date	Illnesses	Date	Operations	Date
○ high blood pressure	_____	○ heart (angina/attack)	_____	○ tonsils	_____
○ high cholesterol	_____	○ asthma	_____	○ appendix	_____
○ kidney disease	_____	○ ulcer	_____	○ gall bladder	_____
○ stroke	_____	○ arthritis	_____	○ grommets	_____
○ epilepsy	_____	○ gout	_____	○ hernia	_____
○ diabetes	_____	○ hysterectomy	_____	○ other	_____
○ cancer (type) _____					

4. Do you smoke?   YES NO
   Do you drink alcohol?   YES NO

5. Have you had any accidents? ? YES NO
   If YES, please list the accidents you have had.

   _____ _____ _____ _____

6. How much exercise do you do in an average week?

Type of exercise (eg walking)	Amount of time per day (eg 30 minutes)	Times per week (eg 3 days/week)

7. Did you have an influenza injection for this season?   YES NO
8. When was your last tetanus immunisation? _____
9. Family history

	Age	Living - illnesses eg blood pressure/asthma/diabetes	Deceased (tick)	Age at death	Cause of death
Father					
Mother					
Brother/s					
Sister's					

10. **For women only:**
    Have you had any pregnancies?   YES NO   If YES, how many? _____
    When was your last cervical smear? _____
    Have you ever had an abnormal cervical smear? YES NO
    When was your last mammogram? _____
11. How did you hear about this medical centre?
    ○ saw an advertisement in the newspaper   ○ recommended by friends or family
    ○ Other _____

Generic Visa Application

(For travel outside Europe)

Please type, or print your answers in ink.

Section 1

If you are applying for a visa as a visitor, for how long do you want the visa to be valid?	
3 months ☐　　　　6 months ☐　　　　1 year ☐　　　　more than 1 year ☐	
Who will be paying for your trip?	
Have you ever been in this country before?	
List dates:	

Section 2

Please tell us your:

Full name. Under line your family name.		
Date of birth	Place of birth. City　　　　　　　Country	
Nationality		
Other names used (maiden, religious, professional, aliases)		
Sex	Marital status	
Male ☐　　　　Female ☐	Single ☐　　Married ☐　　Divorced ☐　　Widowed ☐　　Separated ☐	
What is your father's full name?		
What is your mother's full name?		
What is your passport number?　　　　　　　　Issue and expiry dates		
Place of issue		
Is this your first passport?　　Yes ☐　　　　No ☐　　　　I do not have a passport yet. ☐		

Section 3

Contact details

Your permanent home address	
Your correspondence address, if different.	
Home or mobile telephone number	Fax number
Personal email address	

Section 4

Your Family

If you are married, what is your spouse's full name?
What is your spouse's nationality?
What is your spouse's date of birth?
Where is your spouse now?
Is your spouse travelling with you? (If yes, please note that he/she should complete a separate application form).　　Yes ☐　　　　No ☐

Generic Visa Application

Your Family (continued)

Do you have any children? Yes ☐ No ☐ If yes, please give their details.				
Full name	Date and place of birth	Are they travelling with you?	Yes	No

Section 5

Previous travel	Yes	No
Have you travelled outside your home country?	☐	☐
Have you visited this country before?	☐	☐
Have you applied for a visa for this country before?	☐	☐
Have you ever been refused entry to this country before?	☐	☐
Have you ever been refused entry to another country before?	☐	☐
Have you ever been deported, removed or required to leave this country before?	☐	☐
Have you ever been deported, removed or required to leave another country before?	☐	☐
Have you ever been refused a visa for another country?	☐	☐

Section 6

	Yes	No
1. Do you have any criminal convictions in any country?	☐	☐
2. Have you ever been involved in an act of terrorism or a member of an organisation which supports terrorism?	☐	☐
3. Have you ever been involved in crimes against humanity or war crimes committed in the course of armed conflict?	☐	☐

If you have answered YES to any of the last 3 questions, please give details below.

_____

_____

_____

I certify that I have read and understood all the questions in this application and the answers I have furnished are true and correct to the best of my belief. Any false or misleading statements may result in the permanent refusal of a visa for entry into this country.

Applicant's signature _____ Date (mm/dd/yyyy) _____/_____/_____

© 2009 Aber Publishing – Adult Skills   Forms – Book 1